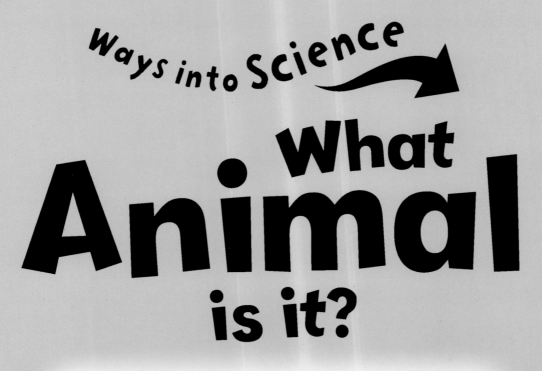

Ways into Science

# What Animal is it?

Peter Riley

FRANKLIN WATTS
LONDON • SYDNEY

Franklin Watts
Published in Great Britain in 2016
by The Watts Publishing Group

Copyright images © Franklin Watts 2014
Copyright text © Peter Riley 2014
(Text has previously appeared in Ways into Science:
What Animal Is it? (2003) but has been comprehensively
re-written for this edition.)

Editor: Julia Bird
Designer: Basement 68

ISBN: 978 1 4451 3478 9
Dewey classification number: 590

Printed in China

Franklin Watts
An imprint of
Hachette Children's Group
Part of The Watts Publishing GroupCarmelite House
50 Victoria Embankment
London EC4Y 0DZ

An Hachette UK Company
www.hachette.co.uk
www.franklinwatts.co.uk

FSC
www.fsc.org
MIX
Paper from
responsible sources
FSC® C104740

Photo acknowledgements: Dreamstime/Alexstar: 12b,
27cr. Dave Allen Photo: 13t. Alptraum: 27crb. Alslutsky 27bl.
Andreanita: 5br, 9b. Anharris 11t. Antrey: 6t. Brad Calkins:
23cl. Chalkovsky: 5tr, 12t. Chasbrutlag: 25t. Crookid: 14c.
Daburke: 9t. Ecophoto: 5crb, 16c. Egal: 23t, 26br.
Electrorowan: 23r, 27c. Enraiha: 4, 8t. Epantha 22c. Four Oaks:
6br. Geddy: 24c. Grimplet: 22b. Hoptrop 25bl. Hsandler: 18b.
Paul Michael Hughes: 26c. Isselee: 20b, 23c, 26bl.
Javarman: 21b. Michael Jung: 6bc. Kcmatt: 7tl. Kharlamova:
16t. Kirsanovv 13b. Kornilovdream: 5bl, 10t. Knorre: 14b, 26bc.
Leyrer: 15b. Chris Lorenz: 7tr. Luiscar: 25br. Mailthepic: 24b,
29b. Mishkacz: 27bc. Mrallen: 11b. Natalyaa 17b, 18t.
Photobudai: 5cr, 21t. Pirita: 7b. Scottbeard: 3, 10b.
Brandon Seidel: 17t. Sikth: 13c. Teekaygee: 24t. Twindesign:
16b. Verastuchelova: 8b, 28b. Jamie Wilson: 25c, 27cb. Yarndoll:
15t. Zateychuk: 20t. Shutterstock/Nantawat Chotsuwan:
front cover t. Eric Isselee: front cover b, 19.
Every attempt has been made to clear copyright.
Should there be any inadvertent omission,
please apply to the Publishers for rectification.

# Contents

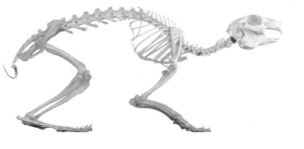

# All **kinds** of **animals**

There are many kinds of animals.

An ant is a tiny animal. You need a magnifying glass to see it well.

An elephant is a huge animal. This elephant is more than twice as tall as a boy.

Some animals have wings and can fly.

Other animals slither along the ground.

Most animals have legs and can walk, jump and run.

What different animals can you think of?

# Animals and food

Animals eat different kinds of food.

Some animals eat only plants. They are called herbivores.
A rabbit is a herbivore.

Some animals eat only other animals. They are called carnivores. A cat is a carnivore.

Some animals eat plants and animals. They are called omnivores. A bear is an omnivore.

What other herbivores, carnivores and omnivores can you think of?

9

# Vertebrates

Lots of animals have bones. The bones join together and form a skeleton. This is the skeleton of a cat.

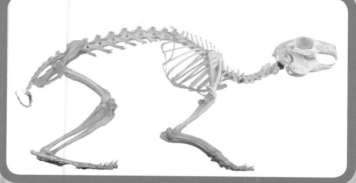

Animals with a skeleton of bones are called vertebrates.

Cats are vertebrates.

Giraffes are vertebrates. They have long necks and legs.

Crocodiles are vertebrates, too. They have long backs and tails.

Some vertebrates have fins. What are they? Turn the page to find out.

# Fish

Fish are vertebrates that live in water. Their fins help them steer through the water. Long, thin bones in their skeleton hold up the fins.

When a fish swims, it moves its body from side to side.

12

Fish are covered in scales.
These protect them from
the water.

scales

Fish all have gills.
Gills let fish breathe
underwater.
They cannot
breathe out
of water.

gills

# Amphibians

Some animals begin their life in water and later live on land. They are called amphibians.

The tadpole looks like a fish and lives in water.

It grows and changes into a frog.

Frogs live on land. They have skin covered in slime.

Toads look like frogs, but they usually have warty skin.

A newt is an amphibian. It has a broad, flat tail.

What animal looks like a newt but only lives on land? Turn the page to find out.

# Reptiles

Lizards look like newts. Lizards live on land and are reptiles.

All reptiles have scales on their body. The tortoise is a reptile with a shell. It has scales on its head, legs and tail.

Some reptiles, like this snake, have no legs.

Turtles are reptiles that live in water. They don't have gills to breathe like fish. They swim to the surface to breathe.

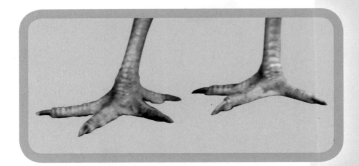

This animal has got scales on its feet. Is it a reptile? Turn the page to find out.

# Birds

beak

feathers

This animal is a bird.

It has got a beak.
It is covered in
feathers. It has got
wings. It has two legs
that are covered in scales.

Birds use their
wings to fly.

Some birds cannot fly. Their wings are too small. The ostrich is a bird that cannot fly.

There are lots of different birds. How many can you think of?

19

# Mammals

Animals with hair are called mammals.

An elephant has only got a few hairs on its skin.

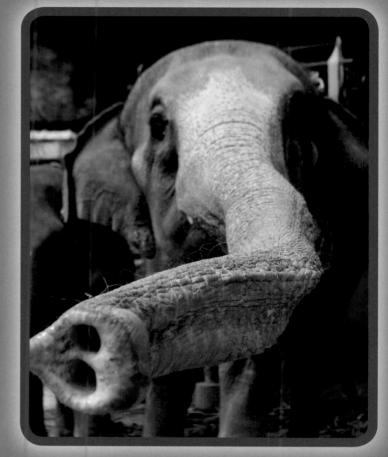

A rabbit is covered in hair, called fur.

Most mammals live on land but some live in water.

Dolphins are mammals that live in seas and rivers. They go to the surface to breathe.

Bats are mammals that can fly.

Lots of animals do not have bones. Can you think of any? Turn the page to find out more.

# Invertebrates

Animals that do not have a skeleton of bones are called invertebrates. Some invertebrates have soft bodies. Earthworms, slugs and snails have soft bodies.

An earthworm has rings of muscles along its body.

feelers

A slug has a thicker body and feelers on its head.

A snail has a body like a slug. You can tell it is a snail because it has a shell.

What are A, B and C?

A

B

C

Some invertebrates have hard bodies. Can you think of some? Turn the page to find out more.

# Hard bodies

There are lots of invertebrates with hard bodies. All of them have got legs with lots of joints. Some have long bodies and lots of legs.

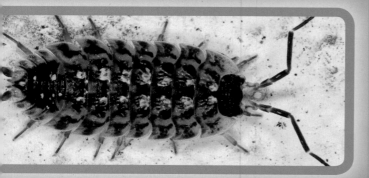

Others have shorter bodies with fourteen legs.

Insects have six legs. Flies are insects with two wings.

Moths are insects with four wings.

A beetle is an insect with wings on its back. The wings are difficult to see.

A ladybird is a beetle. You can only see its wings when it flies.

Spiders are not insects. They have eight legs and no wings.

# Humans

Do humans have skeletons? Are they vertebrates or invertebrates? Which animal group do humans belong to?

Which of these animals belongs in the same group as humans?

A

B

C

# Make a table like this.

| Hair | Scales | Breathe air | Breathe in water | Legs | Animal? |
|------|--------|-------------|------------------|------|---------|
| Yes  | No     | Yes         | No               | 4    | ?       |
| No   | No     | Yes         | No               | 0    | A       |
| No   | Yes    | No          | Yes              | 0    | ?       |
| No   | No     | Yes         | No               | 6    | ?       |
| No   | Yes    | Yes         | No               | 4    | ?       |
| No   | Yes    | Yes         | No               | 2    | ?       |

Look at these animals. Work out where they go in the table.

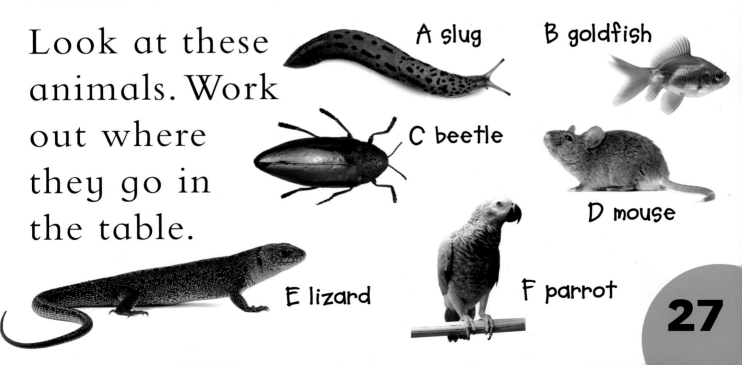

A slug

B goldfish

C beetle

D mouse

E lizard

F parrot

27

# Useful words

**Beetle** – an insect with a pair of hard, tough wings on its back, covering a pair of wings that it flaps to fly.

**Carnivore** – an animal that eats only other animals.

**Gills** – the parts of a fish that let it breathe underwater.

**Herbivore** – an animal that eats only plants.

**Invertebrates** – animals that do not have a skeleton of bones.

**Joint** – a place between two parts of an arm or leg.

**Magnifying glass** – a piece of glass or plastic that makes small things look larger when you look through it.

**Muscles** – parts of the body that help the body move.

**Omnivore** – an animal that eats both plants and animals.

**Scales** – small, hard, flat objects that cover the skin of fish, reptiles and the legs of birds.

**Skeleton** – a part of the body that supports or holds up other parts.

**Slither** – a way of moving on the ground without using legs.

**Tadpole** – the young stage of an amphibian that lives in water and looks like a fish.

**Vertebrates** – animals that have a skeleton of bones.

# Some answers

Here are some answers to the questions we have asked in this book. Don't worry if you had some different answers to ours: you may be right, too. Talk through your answers with other people and see if you can explain why they are right.

**Page 7** There are almost countless answers, but children could start with animals in their neighbourhood, then in the countryside or on a farm, then at a zoo or on television programmes.

**Page 9** Herbivores – cow, sheep, horse, zebra, giraffe, finch, tortoise. Carnivores – lion, wolf, tiger, killer whale, shark, frog, snake, crocodile. Omnivore – pig, squirrel, opossum, chipmunk, human.

**Page 19** There are thousands of types of bird – here are just a few: duck, goose, turkey, finch, robin, sparrow, starling, eagle, hawk, vulture, heron.

**Page 23** A snail; B earthworm; C slug

**Page 26** Humans have skeletons. They are vertebrates. They belong to the mammals group. Rabbits (A) also belong to the mammals group.

**Page 27** The answers are (top to bottom): D mouse, A slug, B goldfish, C beetle, E lizard, F parrot.

# Index

# About this book

**Ways into Science** is designed to encourage children to think about their everyday world in a scientific way, and to make investigations to test their ideas. There are five lines of enquiry that scientists make in investigations. These are grouping and classifying, observing over time, making a fair test, searching for patterns and researching using secondary sources. When children open this book they are already making one line of enquiry – researching about animals. As they read through the book, they are invited to make other lines of enquiry and to develop skills in scientific investigation.

• On page 9 they are asked to group and classify animals into herbivores, carnivores and omnivores.

• On page 26 they are asked to classify humans with rabbits which they may remember as members of the mammal group.

• On page 27 they must use observational skills in identifying animals with scales and legs, and recording skills in filling in a table correctly. You may like to extend the work by setting up a scientific enquiry over time. Ask the children to observe and record the animals they see in their neighbourhood once a week for several weeks. If there are changes in the animals they see, you could encourage them to suggest reasons for the changes and look for an answer about the weather.